*Sin*sation

KLARA COKU

authorHOUSE®

AuthorHouse™
1663 Liberty Drive
Bloomington, IN 47403
www.authorhouse.com
Phone: 1 (800) 839-8640

© 2019 Klara Coku. All rights reserved.

No part of this book may be reproduced, stored in a retrieval system, or transmitted by any means without the written permission of the author.

Published by AuthorHouse 05/31/2019

ISBN: 978-1-7283-1398-6 (sc)
ISBN: 978-1-7283-1397-9 (e)

Print information available on the last page.

Any people depicted in stock imagery provided by Getty Images are models, and such images are being used for illustrative purposes only. Certain stock imagery © Getty Images.

This book is printed on acid-free paper.

Because of the dynamic nature of the Internet, any web addresses or links contained in this book may have changed since publication and may no longer be valid. The views expressed in this work are solely those of the author and do not necessarily reflect the views of the publisher, and the publisher hereby disclaims any responsibility for them.

Dedication

To our past selves, may they always be
a reminder of lessons learned.
To our present selves, may they always
lead us in the right direction.
To our future selves, may they always set the
bar higher every time we catch up.

-klara coku

Acknowledgement

Thank you to everyone who contributed to helping me bring this book to life, whether directly or indirectly. Whether I walked into a coffee shop and watched an interaction happen that inspired me to put pen to paper, whether you helped me get past writer's block by reminding me of my past work, whether you texted me to say let's get a drink because I needed a break, whether you called to check up on my progress, whether you broke my heart, or whether you helped heal it, thank you.

This is for you.

A special thank you goes to my fellow writers, whom, without hesitation, said yes when I asked if they wanted to be a part of my vision in writing a few perspective pieces for the book. Thank you, Victor Ivezaj, George Kocovic, Gjovalin Peraj and Michee Felius, for writing your pieces so beautifully, and letting me bounce off of them. Your work is magical —I am honored to have your words spread throughout this book.

*Sin*sation

Written by: Klara Coku
Illustrated by: Klaudio Coku

she was dangerous
dangerous in that
she lit a spark in every eye that met her gaze
the same gaze that could cut through you like a knife
dangerous in that
she didn't conform to society's standards of behavior
she often made her own rules while breaking everyone else's
she wasn't protected by fear. she was wild, free

a daredevil in the rarest form.

i neglected myself a lot

i let my own self down trying to please everyone else, always putting others first, always more concerned with placing smiles on strangers faces and fulfilling promises to friends. *friends.* what are friends? friends are there when *they* need *you*, gone when they're done. & that was my problem, you know. they left, turned their back one me, hurt me, neglected me, killed me, but i always let them come back. always. the second they needed me again, i let them come crawling back, and with every step they took toward me, i lost another piece of myself. crazy thing is, not one of them ever stopped to help me look for the missing pieces, none of them would lend a helping hand. there when t*hey* need *you*. *r*emember that. i lost sight of that at one point.

i neglected myself a lot.

not anymore.

i'm sorry if there was once a moment in time, an instance when i did not uplift you, say that i like your hair when i thought it fell perfectly along the side of your face, that i enjoyed our conversation, that i thought you had a really good point. i'm sorry if i didn't listen intently, if my mind wasn't fully on you or if you asked me a question and i answered simply to answer it. i'm sorry if i made you feel bad one day about yourself, if i said something negative accidentally (or on purpose, because i was having a bad day myself) and it ruined your whole day. i'm sorry if i didn't help you with something, because i didn't want to inconvenience myself. i'm sorry, to every beautiful, talented, strong, confident, smart female i have come across in my lifetime, for ever making you feel less than. we go through so much, i'm sorry if i ever took part in not uplifting you. i'm sorry.
i know better.

why do you worry so much about how you are perceived by others? how they see you isn't a reflection of you, but rather a reflection of how they feel about themselves. you could be peaceful, but still be seen as agitated by the unrest. be loving, but still seen as cold by the cruel. mindful, but seen as oblivious by the heedless.

my point, my love, is that you will never be seen how you want to be seen to others, you can only control how you see yourself, and if it's anything like i see you, it's pretty goddamn special.

you won't be everything
for everyone
every time
hell ... sometimes
you won't even be everything for you
but you will always

always

be enough.

a glacier where my heart once beat
a volcano of desire amidst a sea of turbulent emotions
memories frozen in purgatory among the ashes of a past life
only she can reignite the spark in my soul.
only she can swim in the ocean of my being
only she can tame the flames of my uncertainty
without the nectar of her existence, mine will surely wither
she is the moon to which the tides of my lifeblood respond
her beauty, her spirit, her aura, her presence
her breath that glimmers with every word
and kindles my spirit into eternity.

g.k.

an ocean turbulent in his departure
his every step a ripple effect in my heart
thoughts of him flooding my very being
a fire burns within me
strong, powerful, immense
like him, only stronger, more powerful, more intense
a force not to be reckoned with
like the wind howling outside your window at 2am
you want to get up and close the window
but you can't bring yourself to
he brought forth a sense of freedom that came with the wind
without him, i wasn't free, i was trapped
only he could take me into eternity
mind, body, soul

k.c.

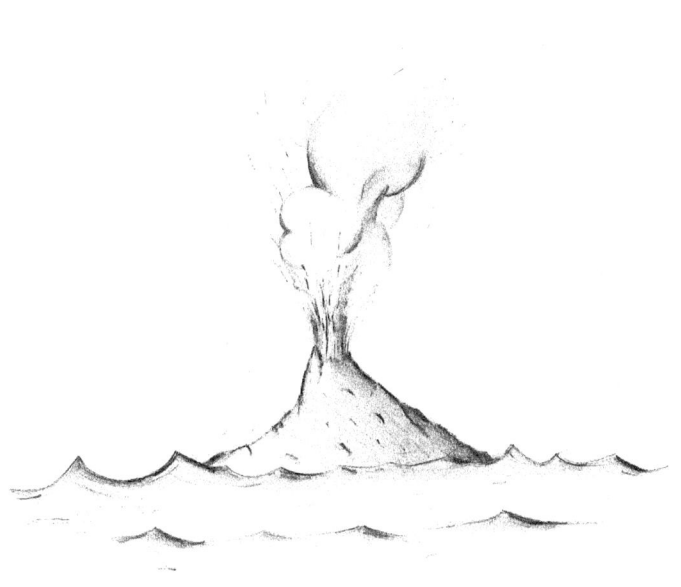

even though i knew it was all over, i still hang on to the idea of us. i know, pathetic, but i do. i can't help but remember who we once were. happy. in love. us. but us faded into him and her, him and her became them, and it killed me. it absolutely shattered me.

and yes, it's okay to show vulnerability. it's okay to break down and cry for someone who you think is worth crying over. it's okay. we all deal with things in our own unique way. but, *fuck*. this shattered me.

i don't know where to start picking up the pieces.

there's a certain rush you get during the first snowfall, isn't there? you look outside your windows, wrapped in a blanket with Christmas trees and reindeer on it, wearing your favorite red and green plush socks while the fireplace radiates all the heat and comfort you can take, sipping on hot cocoa out of your favorite winter coffee mugs.

what about that first day of Spring? i don't mean the official first day, i mean the day you walk outside, and the sky is clean, there's that flower you've been waiting all winter to greet you with it's presence, that breath of fresh air you take without feeling like the crisp air hurt your throat, and that bird, singing because he's so happy to be back.

and Summer. ah. Summer. that first time you sink your toes into the shore to welcome the ocean with open arms, the ice cold beer you crack open on the sand as you lay on your beach towel giving the sun complete permission to turn you seven shades darker, because you've waited all year for this, after all.

Fall. Fall. nothing compares to seeing that first lone leaf turn from green to a crisp orange, the leader of the pack. the most beautiful leaf to cross your path. all of a sudden, your coffee changes flavor for the season, you go from regular black coffee with just a splash of cream, to anything and everything fall; maple, pecan, pumpkin, you name it.

but, something happens in the short time between that first snowfall and the second one, between that first flower bloom to the second one, between that first tan and the second one, between that first orange leaf to that second one. the mood shifts. everything changes. we no longer appreciate it as much. it's nice, but it's not worth thinking about. and that third, fourth, fifth time, it's just life. it's just another day. these things that were once not too long ago appreciated, are nothing short of inconveniences now. just another snowstorm you have to shovel your driveway after, another allergy the freshly bloomed flowers are causing you, another heatwave you'll have to withstand, another leaf you'll have to rake.

sad, isn't it? how God gives us all these beautiful things in life to enjoy, season in and season out, and we barely give it a second chance.

there you go again, hating him
for treating you like a piece of garbage
you can't be mad at what you allow
remember that.

what time is it? no, no, don't look at your watch, that's not what i mean. i mean, what time is it in your life, right now. where should you be? because i know it's not here, not anymore. you've outgrown this place. it's time to move on. this place full of negative energy, this place full of all the lies, all the talking, false promises, bullshit, straight faces, curved responses, the ride or dies who quickly run out of gas, the *i got you's* who quickly turn to *you need me,* this is a never ending cycle in this town, kid. it's your time to leave. explore the world with those beautiful new wings of yours. you've already wasted far too much time here. you're too precious for this bubble. *escape.* do it for the ones that couldn't. do it for the dreamers.

do it for you

for me.

a sea of people, i looked for traits of you in all of them. all of them, but i never succeed, not even close. until one day, i saw your eyes on someone, i swear, i almost approached her. i was going to call her by your name, hug her, just to see if it still felt the same. she caught me staring and my face immediately turned red, so i apologized and started walking away, but she stopped me, looked at me right in the eye and said "it'll get easier, cupcake. i promise." it took me a whole minute to process what she said. i look up, and she was gone, just like that. it's like she vanished into thin air, and i just stood there trying to wrap my head around the fact that you were the only one who ever called me cupcake. my entire life, no one ever called me that, but you. but that was it, you know? that was the day i stopped questioning God, His ways, His plans, why He decided to take you from me, why He thought you should be the one carried away in a body bag that night and not me. i was the one driving. why not me? it made no sense, but i thank you. i thank you for sending her my way to give me some peace of mind. i know those were your eyes staring back at me. i just know it.

until we meet again

i love you, cupcake.

it wasn't the fact that it ended that bothered me
it was *how* it ended that i had a hard time coming to terms with
no note, no text, no call, no explanation, no closure
it's been 281 days
i sit
i wait
i can't move on.

i was the tissue he wiped his crocodile tears with, the blanket that warmed his cold heart, the bulb that shined light into his dark soul. but just like everything else he touched, the tissue became drenched, the blanket ripped, and the bulb dimmed and just like that, he disposed of me. almost as if i never existed, because that was the thing about him, he used people until they no longer benefited him.

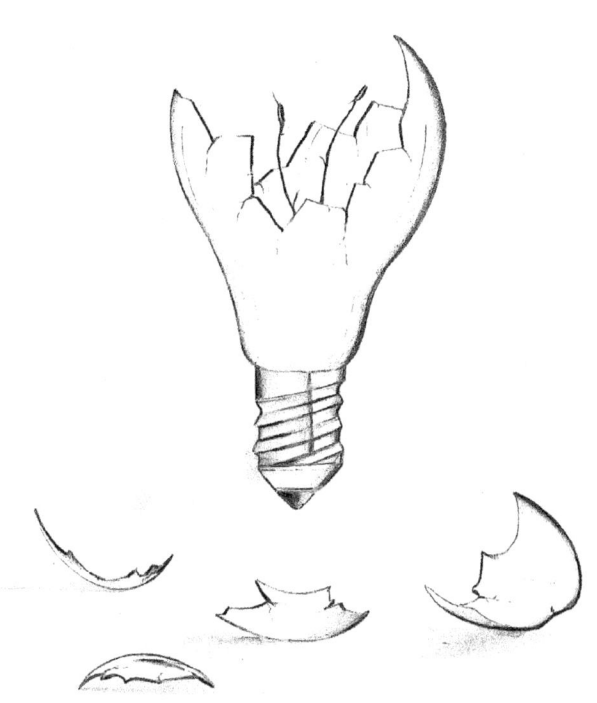

i used to be terrified of monsters
until you turned me *into* one.

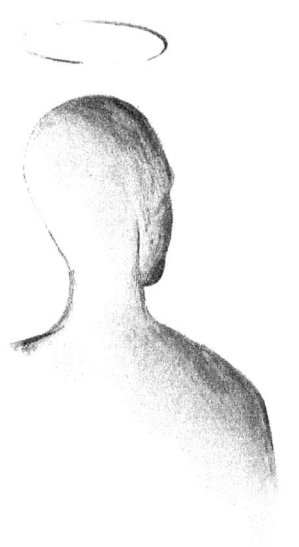
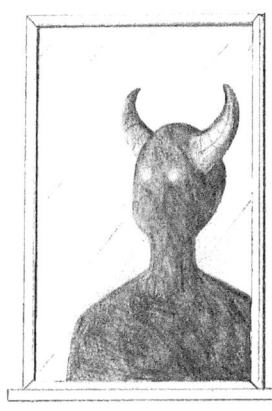

us. the best that never was

the hearts that uncontrollably beat for one another
in sync. yet
could never be
the best that never was
he was the feeling she couldn't shake
the love she found too much to bear
she was the breath he couldn't catch
the spark he couldn't explain.

we didn't last

not due to lack of trying. no
but rather, a realization of over-comfort
they say nothing great lasts forever
and that eventually all good things come to an end
and we were good together

goddamn it, we were so good.

when she was with him
she felt as if
the center of the universe
could be anywhere she wanted it to be.

i imagine no other generation was like ours. i don't know, there's something so strange about us -- the way we don't value anything anymore, things that used to mean something like love, respect, morals, communication. all of a sudden, being stone cold is admired, showing emotion is equal to showing weakness, disrespect is the norm, and god forbid anyone hangs on to their morals, because that would make you unlike everyone else, and we *are* the generation of unoriginality after all.

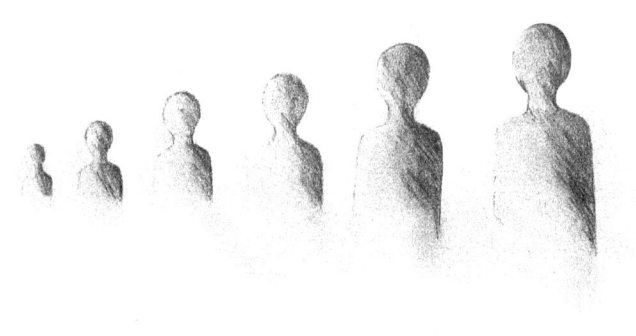

of all the people that have walked in
and out of my life
you're the only one i always looked forward to walking in
and always feared seeing you walk out

please
don't ever walk out.

she haunted him, his reflection on storefront glass turned into her, if only for a split second. he found himself saying things like *bless her heart,* because even though she was born and raised in Brooklyn, she picked it up one summer down South, and she never stopped saying it. he drank wine and beer out of regular glasses because *wine glasses are for trashy girls and beer bottles are for alcoholics.* she was inhabiting his very existence, and he didn't know how to make it stop.

i'm almost at the door, don't let me walk out
call out my name so i can turn around
and we can go back to playing pretend.

in a fast car, bottle in one hand, wheel on the other. momma isn't worried, daddy doesn't care, so hop in, baby. i'm ready to get outta this city. i'll go fast enough to get away quicker. i'll go fast enough to make the memories die faster, fast enough for the wind to fill the empty feeling in your heart, the music loud enough to replace the lies your ears have heard, the scenery beautiful enough to replace the tragedy your eyes have seen.

so hop in, baby. hop in my fast car
i'll go faster so we die sooner.

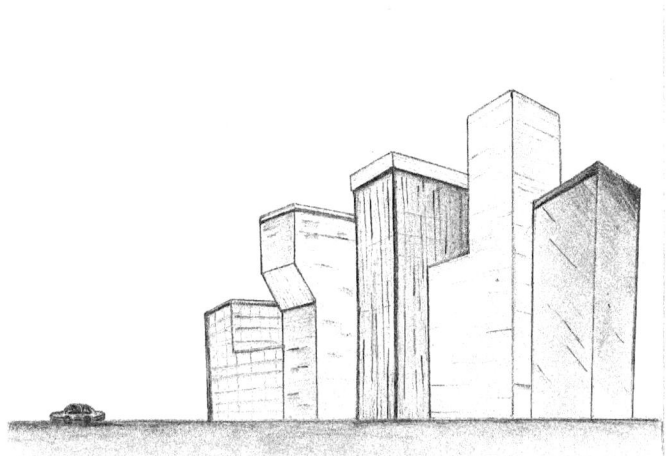

i miss the old days when you didn't have to compete for
people's affection
when you were loved for being you
not for the type of car you drive
how many followers you have on social media
or if you can afford all the latest trends
i miss the old days when people saw hearts
i miss the days when people had *depth*.

even though she was in love
she wrote of sadness
because while her heart was full of joy
she had to prepare her mind for the pain
that would eventually find her.

the worst part is
i can't even blame you for my broken heart
i willingly let myself get to that point
i knew it was coming
but i couldn't help it
you were just so *goddamn* addicting.

& right when you're about to give in
promise me you'll take a deep breath first
breathe your whole entire self in
hold it
hold it
hold it
okay, breathe out
then, ask yourself
do you honestly believe it's going to be different this time?

yeah, me neither.

i know, baby
i know it feels like you'll never fall in love again
but i promise you, you will
someone will walk into your life
and return everything he ever took from you
but that can't happen if you keep shutting everyone out
don't make them pay for his sins
it just isn't right.

he forgot them quicker than he got over them
until he tasted *her*
she was sugar on his lips
and silk underneath his fingertips
but that next morning
she left without a single glance back
and that was when he knew he'd met his match
karma
had finally caught up to him.

when he lost her
he started drinking his vodka straight
because alcohol in his veins was easier to tolerate
than the *pain* in his heart
the *anger* in his soul
the *guilt* in his head.

...and when the dust settles
you will realize that breaking free was inevitable
and that the cracks you heard along the way
was not your heart shattering to pieces
but it was your footsteps
crushing every little piece of your old self
you left behind.

every so often, i'll look at our pictures together and get the urge to rip them apart, to tell that poor little girl to jump out of the frame. she was so innocent, she didn't know what she was getting into at the time. she seems so happy in every single one of them.

i just wanna scream
run
but i can't
it's too late now

the damage is done.

i counted my blessings every day
because i never acted in such a way to deserve them
but they somehow came my way regardless
and for that, i was forever grateful.

oh, but baby, let's not get confused here. you are practically a figment of my imagination, here merely so i have a shoulder to lean on, a name to gasp, a hand to hold, an ear to whisper false promises to, a heart to break.
you're temporary
until he finds his way home.

it was madness the way we fought
and neither one of us would surrender
we started the battle
we lived in a war zone
but the only soldiers on the battlefield
were the two of us.

there was never a dull moment
if we weren't arguing
we were ripping each other apart with silence
and when it was time to pick up the pieces to start all over
we always missed a few and eventually
we became two halves searching frantically
for missing pieces
we didn't realize were long gone
swept away by our very own fucked up idea of *love*.

i spent every night praying to the Lord
to wash away sins i hadn't yet committed
but i knew it was only a matter of time until i did
because i could't escape
and sinning was my only taste of freedom.

i had no intention of leaving, you see. i just needed some time alone to clear my head, organize my thoughts. i was going to come back, i swear i was, but all of a sudden, distance became my friend, distance made me feel things i never felt for you, distance showed me everything i'd been looking for, gave me things i didn't know i wanted, and got rid of all the bad things i didn't know were hurting me. distance saved me from the toxin i was breathing in every night.

distance saved me, *from you.*

-k.c.

distance may have saved you, but it ruined me. while you were gone, i was here waiting for you. the thought of you not making that u-turn brought me unbearable pain. distance was supposed to make you love me harder, not breathe easier, not…i went looking for you, just so you know. i still leave the door unlocked for you, just so you know. whenever i hear footsteps, i stare at the door praying to God it'll be your face i see walking through the door. you see, i was so ready to be better, you should know back then i didn't know any better. your absence is the presence of pain and regret for me.

distance may have saved you, but *it ruined me.*

-m.f.

the crazy thing is
she knew his promises carried no weight
and yet, as soon as he spoke
she acted like he handed her a ton of bricks
because living in denial always *trumped her reality.*

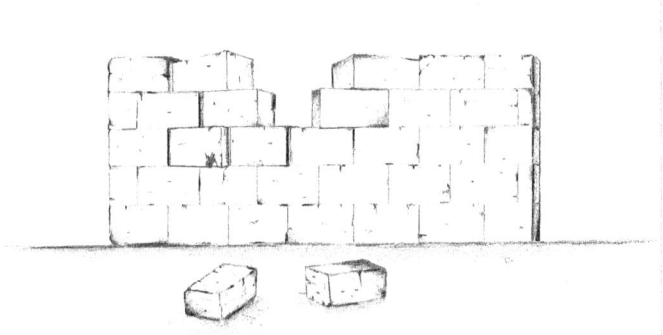

she never felt like she had to explain herself to anyone
her existence knew no boundaries
her actions knew no fear, her free spirit was her defining trait
you saw her as a challenge
and that, my friend
was *mistake number one*
you came in thinking you could confine her
in your four-walled world
mistake number two
you thought you could tame the eccentric
number three.

mama never taught you not to go up against a maverick?

the past isn't worth reliving
you aren't worth forgiving
but i tried
i promise you

i tried.

she beamed sunlight
but her sky blue eyes had always witnessed thunder
i couldn't figure out how she did it
how someone could have gone through hell on earth
and came out of it unscathed; physically, of course
because mentally?
mentally, she lived in an orb
illuminating nothing, but darkness
mentally, she was broken. she was an oxymoron
a walking
living
breathing
contradiction.

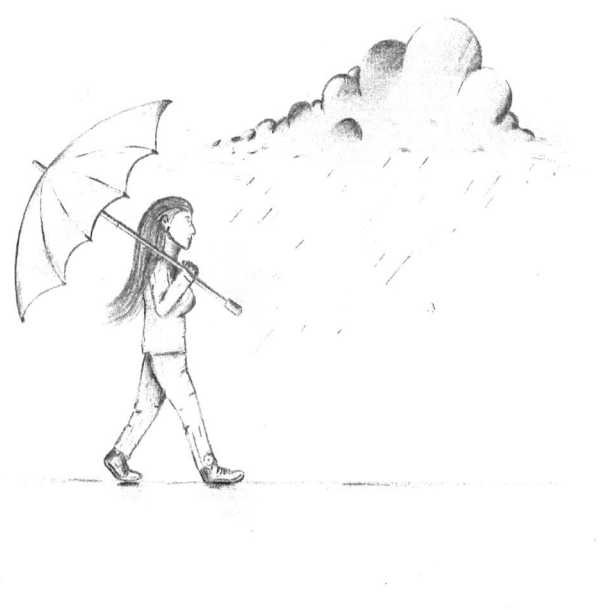

how often we make sacrifices for the wrong people, it's draining, isn't it? especially after a while, you just get so tired. but we keep going, don't we? we keep going, and giving, and saving, and being. being there for all the wrong people, and the worst part is that throughout the whole time, we're neglecting the people we should be focusing on. but they're too nice, they can wait, they won't mind, they'll *get over it,* right?

right?

we never talked about it. we never said the word out loud, i guess we figured if we kept it to ourselves, it would magically go away, but it didn't. obviously. it didn't take long -- seven months, three weeks, and six days to be exact, and on that final day, she looked at me in the eye one final time and said — *please, do not shed another tear for me, i am going to be your angel now, and tears make angels sad. please baby, i am tired of being sad.*

...and my heart shattered into a million tiny little pieces, but i never shed another tear for her again.

fuck my feelings
if you're no longer invested in us
don't waste my time
don't drag this on
because you want to spare me the damage

end it

spare me the damage.

...and then there's the ones you will never learn to stay away from. no matter how many times they do you wrong, you will always go back. as if there's an invisible force always pulling you back in their direction. they will kill your soul, they'll hurt you, they'll mentally abuse you, but you'll be there. you're hurt, sure, but you're so blinded, you can barely feel it. you refuse to let yourself believe that this person you love and care for so much, could hurt you, intentional or otherwise. you tell yourself that's the last time you're reaching out to them, the last time you're sending that text first, the last time you go back. but it won't be, it never is the last time, and that's the way it'll always be, you know?

...and if you're reading this thinking — *well, that's stupid, why would i ever keep going back to a person that keeps hurting me?* — then you're the person doing the hurting. so please, *please*, answer that text, agree to that coffee date, keep in touch, call. because you have the power to save this someone, and i'm afraid they don't have much time left.

he leaned in
looked dead into my eyes, and said
you are so fucking beautiful
and ever since then
there has been a sparkle in my eye
that never goes away.

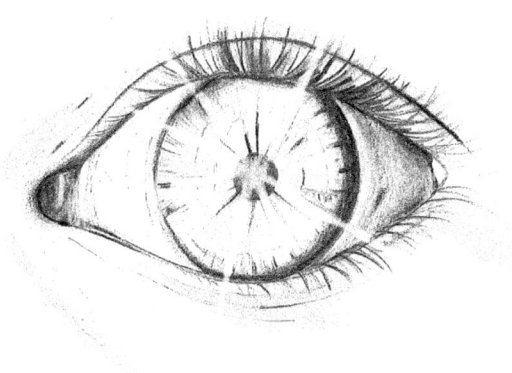

a mixture of drinks
followed by a series of bad decisions
i didn't know how to save myself
and when i turned around to ask you for help
you were gone

probably pouring the next girl
her first glass.

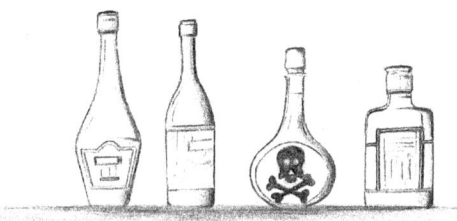

you would've thought i was the cigarette you were smoking. with every puff you took, i got dragged in a little more too, and you see, the crazy thing is, i always thought smoking was a terrible habit, but with you, it just didn't seem to matter. i couldn't help it. you spoke of your dark past with such calmness, such neutrality; it wasn't right, it wasn't wrong, it just ...was. you brought forth a sense of peace about you that i was slowly starting to fall for, and that in itself was a dangerous game. you were a self proclaimed *bad boy gone good,* and i was a self proclaimed *good girl never gone bad,* and i couldn't compete with the past you spoke of, i wasn't interesting enough. hearing you recite stories of those days sent chills down my spine. maybe it was because i always wished i could've been a little more rebellious myself, maybe it was because i was infatuated with every word that escaped your lips, or maybe it was because i was attracted to the idea of wanting someone so outside my comfort zone. whatever it was, it wasn't going away anytime soon. how did i know that? because you did this thing where every time you took one final drag of your cigarette, you almost immediately lit another one, instantly igniting the fire in my eyes all over again at the very strike of your match.

you created the game
you laid out the rules
you taught me how to play
but, somewhere down the line
i became so much better than you at your own game
that the only chance you had of killing your opponent
was cheating.

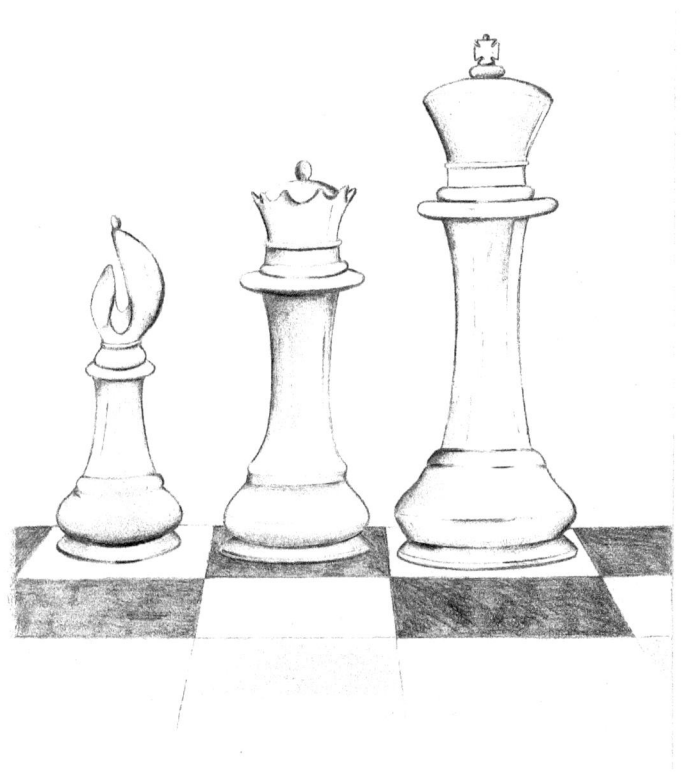

whenever you cross my mind
i can't help but wonder if i cross yours anymore
my solitude was my safe haven
now it's just a place flooded with remnants of you
i tread cautiously, but sometimes, i almost *want* to drown
my solitude was my getaway
now, it's the place i try to get away from
the quiet that i used to enjoy
has all of a sudden become too loud to bear
no peace of mind, only war of thoughts and unanswered questions
was i wrong? is she happy? will we ever meet again?
a constant battle i'll seemingly never win
but one i eventually must conquer - *in solitude*-
missing you... missing a piece of me.

-v.i.

i carry a piece of you with me wherever i go
thoughts of you consume my very being
i thought i was getting better, i really did
but i can't let you go, i'm sorry
i tip toe around things that remind me of you
but then sometimes, i crash right *into* them
accidentally, on purpose
it is the only way i can feel you again
if only mentally, the place you have officially occupied
was i wrong? was he happy? will we ever meet again?
you cross my mind every single day
in case you ever wondered if i think about you
please come find me
i'll complete your missing piece
if you promise to complete mine

k.c.

tell me something

when does it get easier
when does the electricity of your fingertips
ever leave my skin
when does the shape of your lips
ever feel like they're not pressed against mine
when does the sound of your voice
ever stop ringing in my ears
when can i start breathing again
when do i stop drowning

tell me
when?

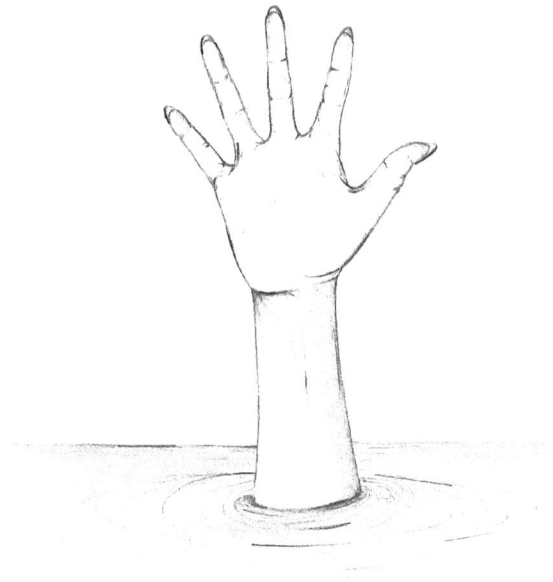

you did what you had to do to kill your sadness
you're not a bad person
you just needed to find ways to cope

to live.

don't feel like you have to entertain anyone
when it no longer feels right
walk away
walk away, but do it right
for God's sake, don't let them wonder why you left
don't be the reason they suffer countless sleepless nights
alone with their thoughts
don't let them wonder where they went wrong
give them peace of mind
even if it means giving them a piece of *your* mind
whether they did you wrong
or you simply got bored
don't just disappear
because no one deserves that mental abuse

trust me.

i stopped praying for a way out
and asked God for an adaptive soul instead
and suddenly, the waters calmed
and i no longer felt like i was drowning.

in too deep
too deep, too late
too much to handle

i risked my own sanity for you
for us. my own one peace of mind
the only place that ever felt safe, you corrupted
it was never enough for you though
you killed us in any and every which way you knew how.

i felt like even my shadow kept it's distance,

that's how afraid of myself i was.

before he left
i used to drink my coffee unsweetened, *black*
now, i find myself adding milk and sugar to every cup
it's the only way I feel i can gain some sort of control
over the bitterness and darkness he left behind.

his actions never matched his intentions
and he never did quite figure out how to get them to line up
it was almost as if his body
refused to cooperate with his heart
and i was always more of an *actions speak louder than words*
kind of girl
and his actions didn't only speak

they screamed

i never learned to rise above the noise.

your grip loosened
more and more each day
and i finally realized
your arms were no longer
my safe haven.

he lit the fuse
and when he tried to save us
from the fire he created
he choked on his own smoke
he was both the arsonist and the firefighter
but it doesn't work that way baby

you have to pick a side.

i never understood how you had the heart to ruin her
physically, emotionally, spiritually, mentally
and then just
vanish
do you know how scarred you left her
do you know she winces at the slightest thought of you
do you even care
Jesus, do you even still remember what her face looked like
or is it just another catch in your sea of battered lovers?

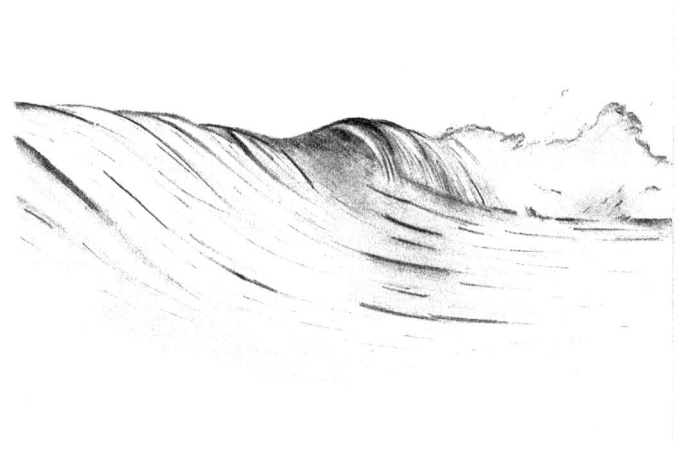

when i felt us drifting apart
i wrapped my arms around you a little tighter
in the hopes that it would keep you a little closer
a little while longer
but, it didn't
i loosened my grip when i realized
holding on hurt more than letting go.

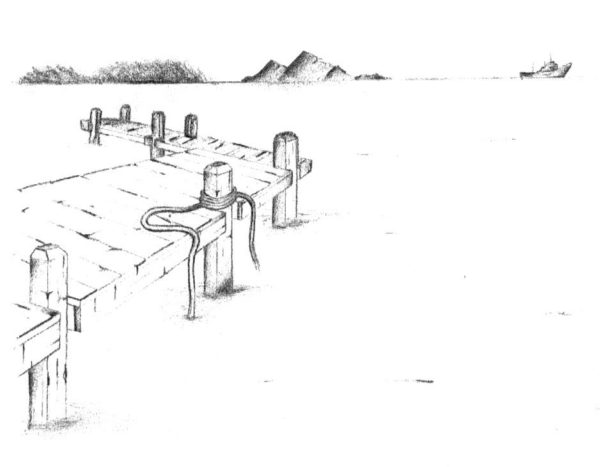

they will kill your soul with their own two hands
and then wonder why they're covered in blood
they will knock you down when you're at your most high
and then wonder why the landing hurt so much
they will throw shade on your name
and then wonder why there's no sun
they are everywhere

there is no escape.

go find your peace. *go*
go read a book
say a prayer
take a walk in the woods
throw pebbles in the ocean
listen to the rain
no. better yet
stand outside in the rain
let it wash over you
let it rid you of all the negatives
you have allowed to consume your entire being
let the rain cleanse you

free you.

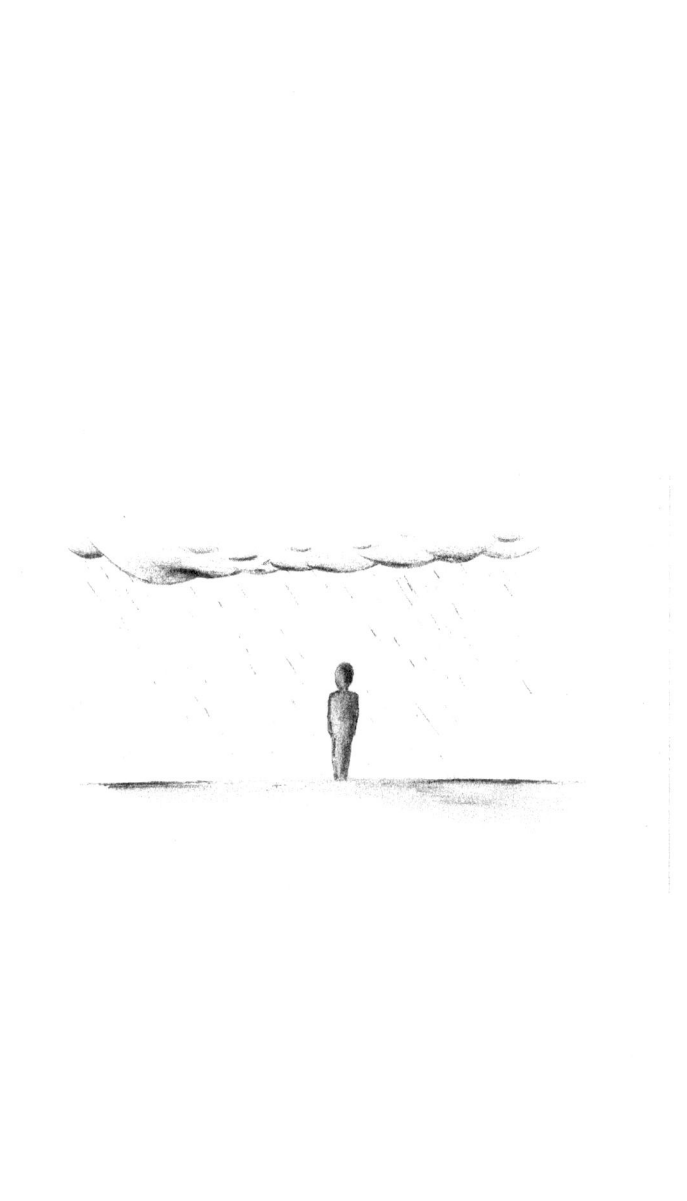

there was both a touch of sorrow and anger when i placed my hand where her heart beat. it's as if she became frozen in time. she proceeded onwards physically, but emotionally seemed as if she kept herself in a past timeline. empty bottles of wine spread across her bedroom floor. crumbled up tissues colored with different shades of make up lined towards her garbage pail. sadly, she seemed broken to me. everything around her gave me the thought of her giving up. why would i choose to pursue any ounce of love with her, to fix the unfixable? as i felt the need to question her, question us, she laid her head on to my shoulder and softly reached for my arm. she had her moment of happiness, and i felt my moment of clarity. she was worth it all. to me, she *was* it all. she needed me, and i wanted her.

-g.p.

numb. that is how i am feeling. anger, sorrow, where my heart once beat, now frozen. physically, i am here, mentally, emotionally, i am back in time. back to that *dark* time. the wine isn't helping propel me forward. i reach for another tissue, the shade of makeup slightly lighter this time as it all fades from my face. i am broken, i am so close to giving up, i am so close. why are you here? you can't fix the unfixable. i am giving up, just please let me lay my head on your shoulder one last time. your arm, it feels safe, it feels like home. stay. for a little while longer, i might stay a little while longer too. i'm smiling. i need you, i want you.

-k.c.

her 24 year old eyes had seen 100 years worth of pain
and yet, she opened them up everyday
and put a smile on her face
with the hope that today would be the day
she finally saw something worth staying *alive* for.

how often do you think about him?
    once?
        twice?
            three times?
                all the time?

what do you think about most? let me guess
    his smile

        his touch

            his laughter

                his eyes

do you go back and read his texts over and over?
the *good morning* ones especially, right?
right.

what do you think he's doing right now?

the same.

neither of you ever learned to love.
neither of you ever learned to leave.

don't love me
if i'm going to be your second priority
don't even love me
if i'm going to be your first
love me when i become a lifestyle
not another number on your list of prime concern.

maybe

you're still shattered

and maybe

that's why you feel the need to write all the time
hoping that one day someone will relate to your words
and help you piece your soul back together
but until then
you will continue to let your pen
bleed onto tear stained paper.

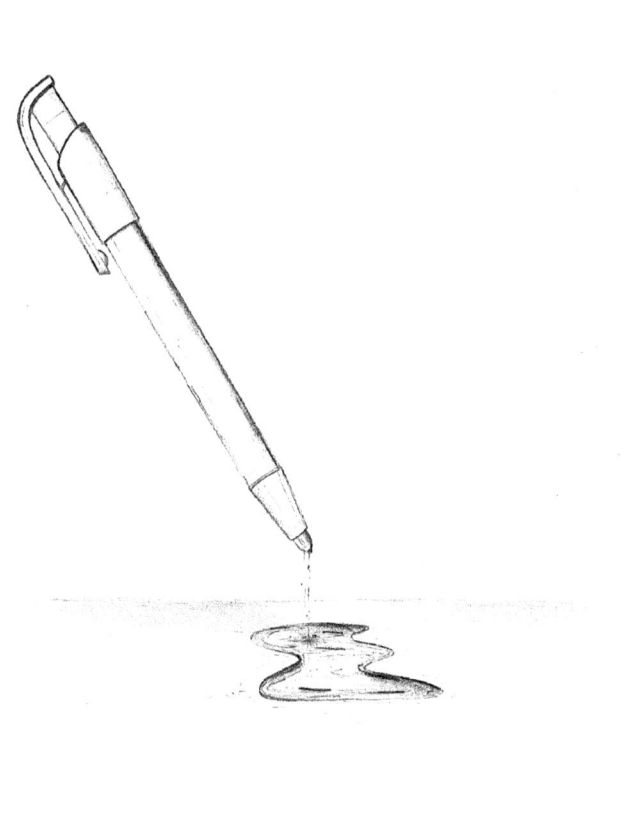

his heart
was where all monsters went
to be created.

the moment we locked eyes
i knew you'd be the one
i would spill my soul on paper for.

isn't the person who ends the relationship
supposed to hurt a little less
if so, then why does my heart feel like it's been ripped out
of my chest
the break i thought i needed from us
turned out to be the very thing that is slowly killing me
and of course, my ego won't let me reach out to you
and tell you any of this
i want to let you know how i made a mistake
i want to let you know i want you back
i'm sorry for hurting you
i'm sorry i didn't take your feelings into consideration
i'm sorry i was selfish
i'm sorry

stupid ego.

if you'd let me go when I wanted to
you wouldn't be going through the pain
of losing me now
you could've gone through it with me
years and years ago
when i decided to let go

don't worry though
it gets better.

my silence wasn't a reaction to your sick attitude
your harsh remarks
your condescending tone
your inconsiderate self
it wasn't because i wanted to give you the cold shoulder
to show you how angry you made me
no. my silence was my peace
the one thing you couldn't fuck with
the one thing you couldn't control
the one thing you could not *take away from me.*

i didn't realize
how much you'd been pulling
in the opposite direction
until i let go
and when i did
i fell so hard
i couldn't get back up.

my biggest fear
was always
someone getting deep inside my head
deep enough to know
just how *troubled* i really was.

it always felt as if
nothing about them being together
ever made any sense
but then she left
and all of a sudden
getting her back was the only thing that mattered
he realized then that all the confusion
was simply *clarity, masked as chaos.*

i raised a glass to your departure.

it's crazy how you have the ability to fuck with my mind
like, i never know where we stand
one day, we're just perfect
but will hardly talk for the next three
you'd think that would be enough for me to say
fuck it, i'm leaving
but that's the thing
it's that *one* day
that one good day
and that's all i need

pathetic.

you will always search for me
everywhere you go
you will always search for me
you'll look for my shade of lipstick on coffee mugs
through dirty coffee shop glass
you will always look for my footprints in the snow
during those brutal winter nights
and for my shadow on concrete
in the hottest of summer days
you will search for my soul
when looking into her eyes
you will always search for me
everywhere you go
you will search
but *you will never find me.*

did you love him?
the one who made you so bitter
so angry at the world
you must have loved him
otherwise
why else would you have allowed him to crush your soul
in such a terrible way
what a shame
such a beautiful soul you used to have.

i hope karma is just a word
someone who had been really wronged made up
to make themselves feel better
i hope it doesn't exist
i hope, for your sake
that it isn't real

& if it is real, well then
for your sake, i pray it has *mercy*.

i guess you figured i'd stop loving you
when you stopped loving me
but it doesn't work that way
my brain knows the truth

but my heart still beats for you.

i've been told
i don't fit in
i don't party enough
i don't wear enough makeup
i don't dress in the latest trends
i read too much
i write too much
i think too much

if you ask me though
i think
they just don't know how to stand out
but then again

what do i know?

i felt like i was trapped in a glass
house full of my own thoughts
and while everyone was able to see the fatality forming
no one was willing to pick up a stone to save me, *from myself.*

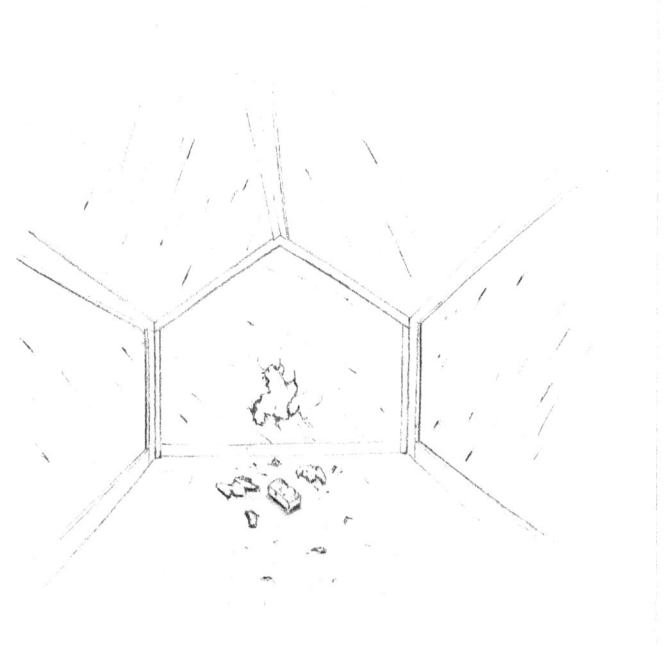

he was
the most powerful form
of self-destruction.

i could sit here and tell you all the ways it eventually gets better, how he'll be nothing, but a memory soon, long gone and forgotten, how you won't think about him as much as the time goes by, how everyday things won't remind you of him as often, and i would be right. don't get me wrong, a small piece of you will always be missing, and the best part is, you will know exactly where to find it, but you will also know, that you will never, *ever* go back to get it, and that will be the most liberating feeling of all.

no matter how many times
i try to exhale the last of you out of me
i fail.
i imagine my lungs look something like that
of a habitual smoker
except mine didn't turn black due to tar
mine turned black to match your soul.

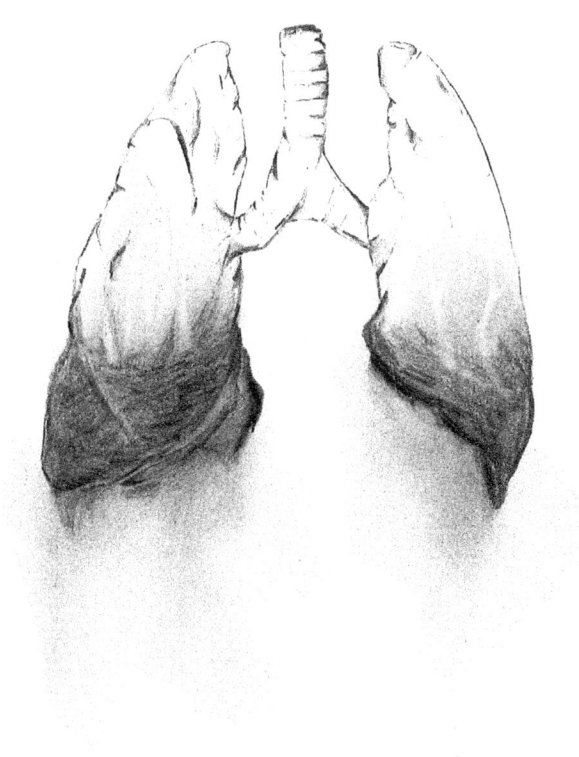

he wiped my tears
but refused to acknowledge
who caused them.

his influence on the opposite sex was almost unbelievable unless you witnessed it with your own two eyes. females melted in his presence. the slightest hint of a smile warranted butterflies and clammy hands. with all that, came a reputation so promiscuous, it made me wonder why i wasted my time. maybe, i liked the attention. maybe, i took pride in knowing someone with such an indisputable reputation took the time to look my way twice. maybe, i needed the validation. whatever it was, i couldn't get him off my mind, and if that meant being just another notch in his belt, *then so be it.*

-k.c.

yes, i admit it, i had a reputation for days. i wish i didn't. i wish i could play the victim and say it was all rumors, but the truth was, they weren't. i was well aware of the influence i had on females, and very often i acted on it, more often with little to no emotional attachment. until i saw her. the only one to make me look twice. i knew she knew exactly who i was, so i wasn't sure why i was wasting my time. maybe i liked her attention, maybe i took pride in thinking my indisputable rep didn't get in the way, maybe i needed her validation. whatever it was, i couldn't get her off my mind, and if that meant spending all my time proving to her that she will never be just another notch on my belt, *then so be it.*

-m.f

every time i think of your name
a smile spreads across my face
and my eyes light up
i never knew your absence
could bring me so much joy.

for this, i thank *you*.

talk to me
tell me things i need to say
to make you see yourself
the way i see you.

sometimes

it's okay to be the one
who got played in the relationship
it makes you wiser
more observant
less caring
tougher
darker
you need those things to survive
you just didn't know it yet.

it's been said
that only one devil fell from the sky
but I believe there were two
because we were once a match made in heaven
but then *crashing down* you flew.

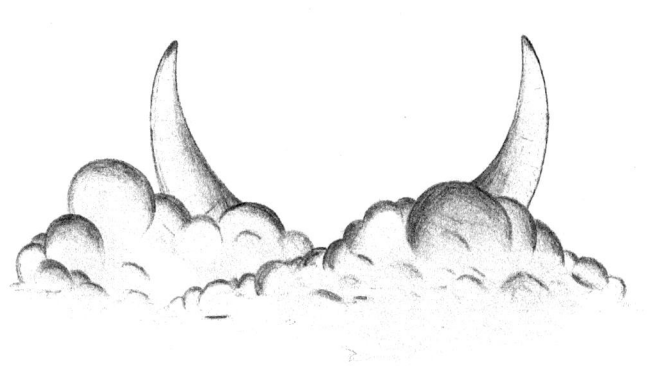

take my hand
lead me anywhere
guide me outside of my mind

there's demons here.

it was never about the unanswered texts, or the silent dinners, or the nights you stumbled home drunk. those never mattered to me. as a matter of fact, i looked forward to my phone not lighting up with your name, the dinners you left me alone to my thoughts, the nights you crawled into bed and fell into a deep vodka induced sleep. that was the thing, i yearned for them, because the more often they happened, the easier you made it for me to pick a fight. i needed reasons, excuses, arguments. i was a coward, i needed ways out. i could never bring myself to tell you just how out of love with you i had fallen. you'd walk inside the house, and my mood instantly changed, you'd touch me, and my skin would crawl, you'd speak, my ears would bleed. i don't know if i will ever be able to put into words what my heart felt for you, but i guess i can stop trying now, because you're no longer here, and my heart is at peace. it hardly thinks of you, but on the rare occasion that it does, the crack my heart suffered comes slightly undone, and it bleeds *black*.

i hope one day
everything will make sense
and maybe
just maybe
i will finally understand
how you managed to destroy us

                     with silence.

thursday, february 15, 2012
3:15pm

there she is again. she picks up a red rose on her way to the bench. she sits, staring at the rose, admiring it, completely oblivious to the fact that she is on the receiving end of that look. she looks up. *holy shit.* she saw me. i look down. all of a sudden, i'm looking at a white pair of flip flops, and a silver ankle bracelet with a seahorse charm hanging from it. i don't know if i'm supposed to look up now. i've been staring at her feet for too long. i don't mind. okay, snap out of it. *hi.* fuck, her voice is so angelic. *hi.* of course, my voice is shaky and awkward.

i look up. she's staring back.

thursday, october 23, 2014
10:23am

i'm staring down at my shiny black shoes, far too fancy if you ask me, but today, for her, i didn't mind. today, my best friend becomes my wife. all of a sudden, white fabric surrounds my black shoes. a vision. an angel. God, she must look so beautiful.

i look up. she's staring back.

thursday, november 12, 2015
11:12pm

i'm stating down at my white sneakers. i'm so stupid. haven't i had enough of white by now? these fucking white walls. fuck these walls. her machine beeps loudly. no. not now. not yet.

i look up, except this time, she isn't staring back.
this time, the heavens got that honor.

i always prided myself in being one of those girls who wouldn't tolerate being with someone who made her feel like she was riding a never-ending roller coaster. then, i met you, and all of a sudden, excuses became acceptable, my feelings started to take the backseat, and i was perfectly okay with that. i was willing to self-destruct as long as i didn't disappoint you. i just couldn't bear the thought of giving you a single reason to leave me.

i know better now.

i pictured it differently. i thought i was going to hear the cracks form in my heart, and the ice freeze the blood in my veins. but none of that happened; not all at once, at least. turns out, my heart was already in pieces, and my veins already frozen, i just didn't realize it was happening all along, because you tricked me by calling my pain, *love.*

i asked you to be the inspiration
behind my every poem
now i've got endless pages dripping of
pain
hurt
suffering
darkness

that's not the inspiration i meant.

the best thing you can do for yourself
is to learn to let go
grudges, lost love, past, anger
let it go
free yourself
save your soul.

it was heartbreaking, watching her live the way that she did. she turned the other cheek at every stare, she winced at every compliment, she froze at the slightest touch, and so when he begged her to let him be her paradise, she ran. it's you, you did this to her. you belittled her to the point where you made her feel like she isn't worthy of anything real, pure, true.

it's you
you did this to me
i mean her.

we tried to leave some things alone
the little things especially
those are the things that cause the most fights
you know?
somehow, all of those little things created chaos
chaos neither one of us knew how to find our way out of.

as she laid on his chest
matching her breathing to his
he couldn't help but notice
how soft her skin was
how effortlessly
his fingertips brushed along her back
how beautiful she was
how lucky he was.

you begged me to stay
on days i made it clear i was looking for a way out
you pushed me away
on nights i was trying to make it work
i'm sorry
you didn't know any better
i'm sorry
you ruined us
i'm sorry
i hate you
but most of all
i'm sorry
you hate you.

there is nothing more painful
than watching the living
dead.

we tolerated to stay
we liked to love
we shut down to keep the peace
we laughed to feel alive
we spoke to not drown in the silence
we did everything
we could
to not suffer the consequences of deterioration
we did everything
we could
to live a lie
and *goddamn* we were so good at it.

you laugh at my pain
i feel the vibrations
cut deep into my bones
and yet, i still pray for you
because one day your heart will ache
as much as mine
and those vibrations?

oh, sweetie
those vibrations
will kill you slowly.

how do you say what can't be said? how do you rid your body of shame. your body, that once stood as a temple is now in shambles. how do you raise your voice after it's been stripped away from you? how do you make them understand that alcohol in your veins doesn't translate to corruption of innocence? of purity? how do you escape your own thoughts? do you ever go back to being able to separate nightmare from reality, or will they always be intertwined from now on? do you ever stop seeing his grim face flash before your eyes, or will he always be there as a reminder of all the sins you can't unsee? do you ever smile anymore? do you ever love, feel, want, breathe anymore?

please, answer me

i don't know how to live anymore.

cocky wasn't the word
it was bigger than that
a certain arrogance i couldn't help, but admire
she walked with all the confidence in the world
she was phlegmatic
she knew her ego couldn't be shaken
a form of self love not to be fucked with
it was the most beautiful thing
i had ever witnessed.

he had carefully planned and calculated
his every move from the beginning
he knew exactly what he was doing
he played such a good game
it almost made me admire him

i said almost.

what you endure
is a reflection of your strength
what you tolerate
is a reflection of your weakness

know the difference.

as i sit and watch him play the piano
i imagine what his fingers would feel like against my skin
stroking me softer than the melody he was creating
gripping me tighter than the gaze on his keys
our bodies in sync to the music floating in the air
with every effortless note he hit
he looks up and my reflection off his dark rimmed glasses
is staring back at me
silently letting me know
that he will never make love to me
the way he does to music.

i'm the writer
i'm supposed to be able to put into words
everything i'm feeling
everything he put me through
i should be able to convey on paper
the ache placed in my heart
but i couldn't
not this time. not with him
nothing was coming to me

how do you portray
the living dead.

we lasted so long
because we kept finding new ways
to fall apart.

he stripped you to your core
and while your body withered in pain
your voice remained silent
for years and years
and when you finally found your voice again
it was barely a crack

hush up, little darling
you're in his world now.

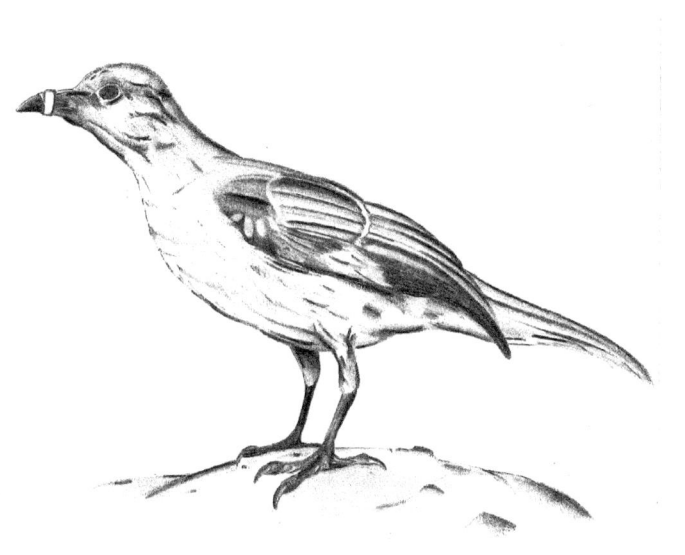

i've heard about you
i know you're lethal
and i know you've heard about me too
but tonight
let's give into our unspoken desires
let's line our actions with our body language
and in the morning
let's pretend it never happened
and we'll leave the regret behind

in the sheets.

it was nights like these
i yearned for his arms
wrapped around my shoulders
but he was gone
and you?
well, your arms always suffocated me
and myself?
well, i never did quite learn
how to make wise decisions.

there is something so fascinating about being broken
we pride ourselves in having experienced something that left us shattered
it's almost as if we love the fucked up beauty that comes with it
with knowing that someone was so close to destroying us
but we stopped them just in time to still hang on to the pieces
so deep they shattered us
but not deep enough to end us.

she said

tonight i want you to make me relive
every ounce of pleasure i have ever felt.

he said

baby, my job is to make you forget
you ever experienced anything else before me.

his smile made every cell in my body
forget their functions
my throat closed up
my heart stopped beating
my lungs stopped breathing
he was the only person who could make me feel
both dead and alive *at the same goddamn time.*

you always did have a habit
of kissing the feet
of those who stomped on you.

they were chaotic greatness
i mean how else would you describe two people
so good for each other
so right that when their bodies clashed
the world fell at their feet
every force of nature was rooting for them
except one
time
time wasn't on their side
time was their biggest enemy
they couldn't be, shouldn't be
time wasn't their friend
they only met to realize what life could've been
should've been

chaotic greatness.

God placed a great burden on us, *the writers*. we not only spill our own souls on paper, but we fill the emotional emptiness others carry. we are the voice others have muted, shut out, or simply didn't know they had, to express the feelings they didn't know how to express. we feel for you— for us —on a different level. unlike most people, we see our pain in our own handwriting scribbled across a white sheet of paper, a napkin, the inside of our hands, anything we can find to write it down on, immortalize it, hold on to it, and get it out there in the hopes that someone, somewhere, reads it

and it *saves* them.

& when i'm no longer around
and they ask about me
just tell them my soul was simply too old for my body
that i had no choice, but to set it free
they'll understand.

the end.

Thank you for giving me a voice.
May my words help you, heal you.
May my words stay with you always.

Love,
Klara

Contact author

Email:klaracoku91@gmail.com
Instagram: klarac91

www.ingramcontent.com/pod-product-compliance
Lightning Source LLC
Chambersburg PA
CBHW071537220526
45469CB00003B/818